FOLDING STEPS

A	D	E	F	T	P 3
H	K	X	Y	I	P 5
U	V	M	W		P 7
C	O	G	Q		P10
P	R	J	L		P12
B	S	N	Z		P14

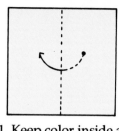

1. Keep color inside and fold paper in half.

G000061137

◀ Watch the fold.

A1

D1

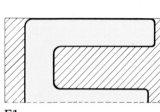

E1

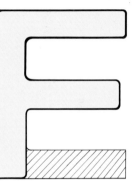

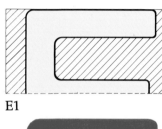

F1 Cut off the "E" shaded portion to make the "F "

A2

D2

E2

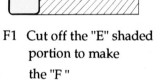

T1

T2

F2

4

FOLDING STEPS

A	D	E	F	T	P 3
H	K	X	Y	I	P 5
U	V	M	W		P 7
C	O	G	Q		P10
P	R	J	L		P12
B	S	N	Z		P14

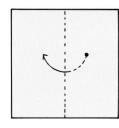

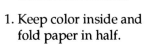

1. Keep color inside and fold paper in half.

2. Follow the K, Y, I patterns below

3. Fold 2 in half. Follow the H and X patterns.

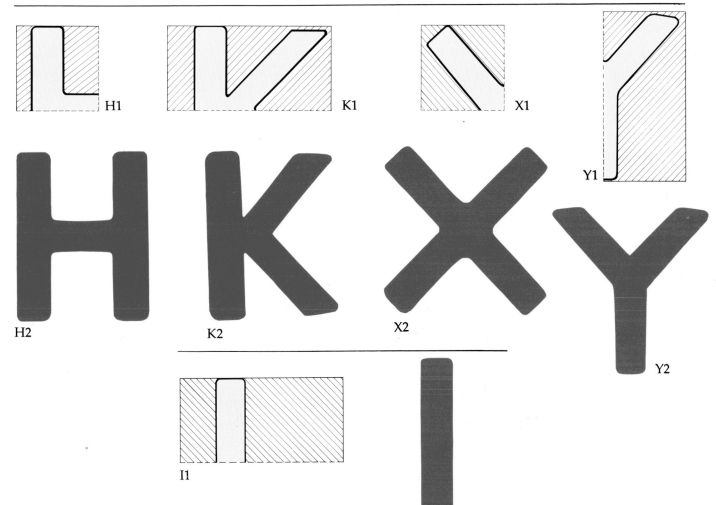

H1

K1

X1

Y1

H2

K2

X2

Y2

I1

I2

Round the corners of the letter to make smooth transitions.

▶Watch the fold   5

FOLDING STEPS

A	D	E	F T	P 3
H	K	X	Y I	P 5
U	V	M	W	P 7
C	O	G	Q	P10
P	R	J	L	P12
B	S	N	Z	P14

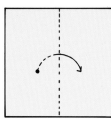

1. Keep color inside and fold paper in half.

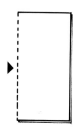

2. Follow the U, V, M, W patterns below.

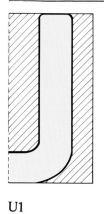

U1

V1

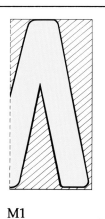

M1

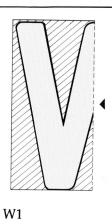

W1

U2

V2

M2

W2

U1, V1, M1, W1 Cut off the shaded area and open to see U, V, M, W letters.

▶Watch the fold   7

Having learned how to make the alphabet in Kirigami, you may now practice creating other lively letter patterns.

FOLDING STEPS

A	D	E	F	T	P 3
H	K	X	Y	I	P 5
U	V	M	W		P 7
C	O	G	Q		P10
P	R	J	L		P12
B	S	N	Z		P14

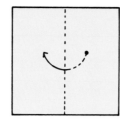

1. Keep color inside and fold paper in half.

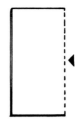

2. Follow the G, Q patterns below

3. Fold 2 in half. Follow the C and O patterns.

◀ Watch the fold

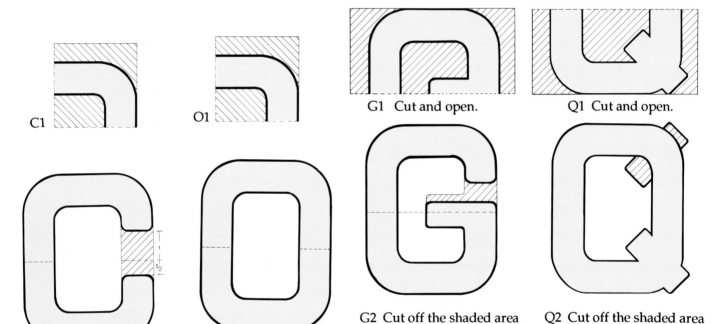

C1

O1

G1 Cut and open.

Q1 Cut and open.

C2

O2

G2 Cut off the shaded area of "G2".

Q2 Cut off the shaded area of Q2 to complete the "Q."

10

C3

O3

G3

Q3

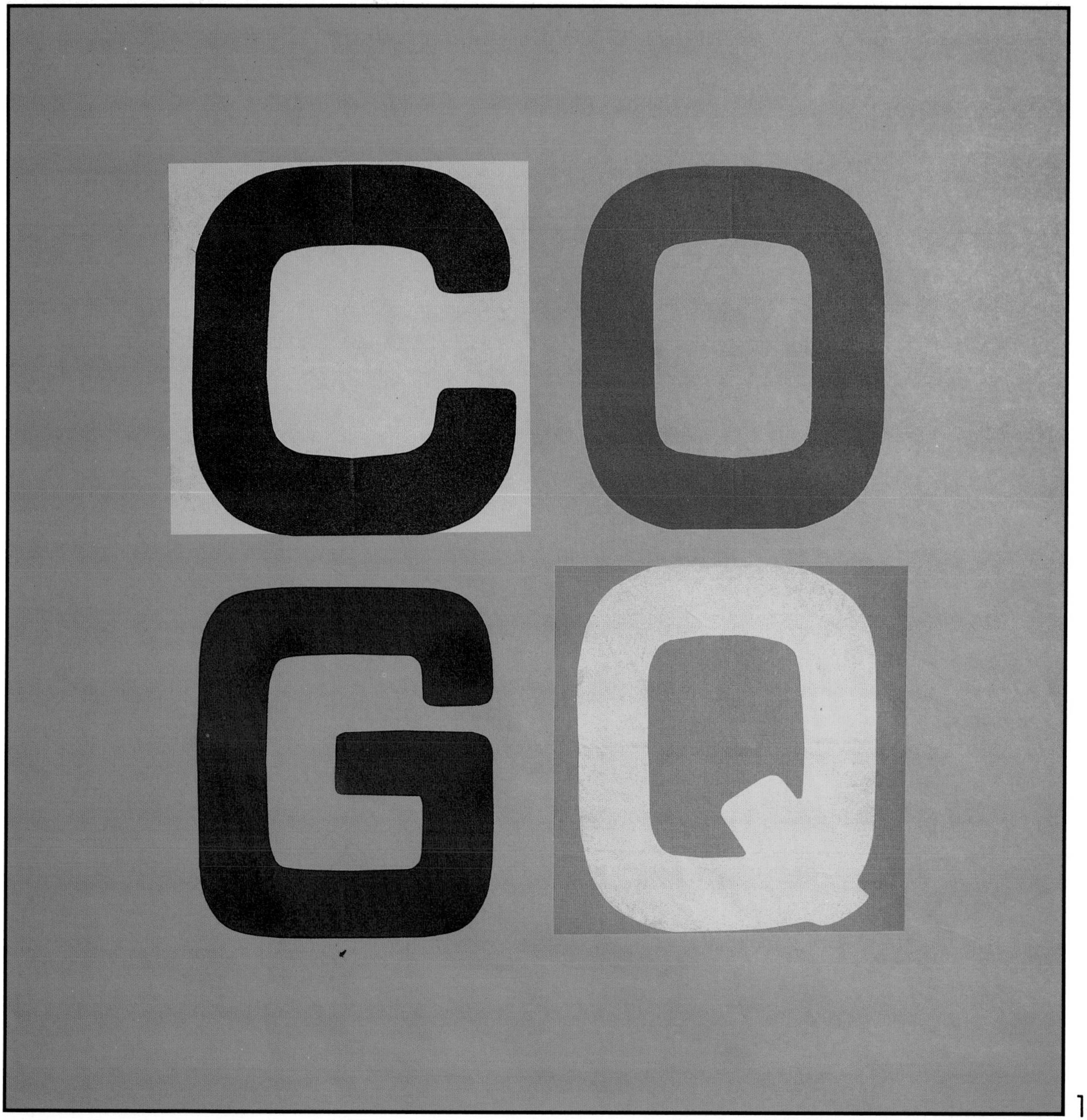
C O
G Q

FOLDING STEPS

See page 14 for chart of folding steps

1. Keep color inside and fold paper in half.

2. Follow the P,R,J,L patterns below

◄ Watch the fold.

P1 P2 P3

R1 R2 R3

J1 L1

J2 L2

J3 L3

To cut P,R, J, L, is somewhat similar. First cut the symmetrical parts then the shaded areas as in P2, R2, J2, L2.

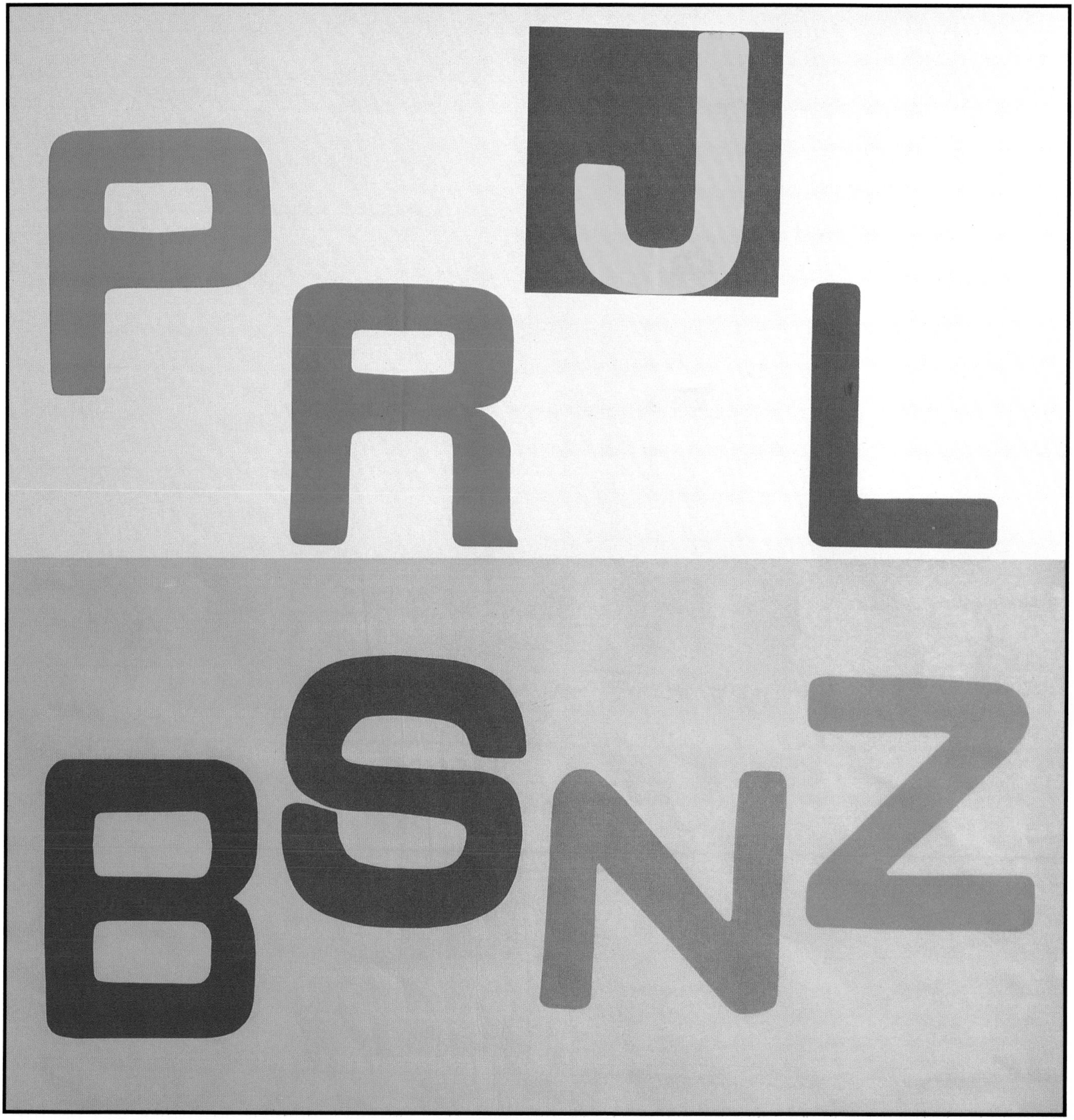
J
P
R
L
B
S
N
Z

B1. Cut D form first and do not open.

S1. Cut off the shaded areas and open.

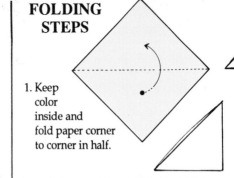
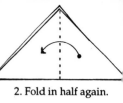

1. Keep color inside and fold paper corner to corner in half.

2. Fold in half again.

3. Ready for "N" and "Z" patterns Below.

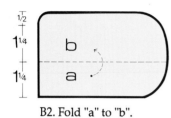

½
1¼
1¼

b
a

B2. Fold "a" to "b".

PATTERNS (Reduced)

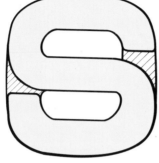

S2. Cut off the shaded areas of S2 to form the S.

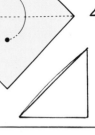

N1. Cut off the shaded areas and open.

Z1. Cut off the shaded area and open.

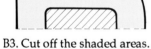

B3. Cut off the shaded areas.

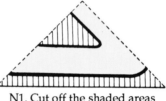
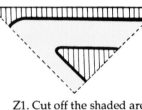

N2. Cut off the shaded areas of N2 to form the N.

Z2. Cut off the shaded areas of Z2 to form the Z.

S3

B4. Spread open to see B.

"B" and "S" folding steps: please see page 10.

N2. Cut off the shaded areas of N2 to form the N.

Z2. Cut off the shaded areas of Z2 to form the Z.

FOLDING STEPS

A D E F T	P 3
H K X Y I	P 5
U V M W	P 7
C O G Q	P10
P R J L	P12
B S N Z	P14

N3

Z3

14